The
Boy
Inside

Lisa Pieri Foster

Copyright © 2022 Lisa Pieri Foster
All rights reserved.
ISBN: 979-8-9855041-3-2

with supervision from Scotchwood Hill Publishing Service

DEDICATION

My mother is the strongest woman I know. She taught me by example that even through the toughest times in life it is possible to stay strong and thrive.

My husband of almost 29 years is truly my Knight in shining armor. He has loved me unconditionally and has always encouraged me. Thank you, sweetie, for always loving me and believing that anything is possible.

CONTENTS

	Acknowledgments	i
	Prologue	1
1	A Rough Beginning	5
2	Kindergarten and Other Adventures	11
3	It's Autism? What a Relief.	16
4	Advocating for an Education	22
5	Scott's Place	25
6	Germany Again	28
7	Why Me?	31
8	Reunited	37
9	Graduation	41
10	The Nightmare Begins	44
11	The Nightmare Continues	49
12	Nowhere to Turn	53
13	Institutionalization	56
14	After Effects	59
15	Lesson Learned	64
	Afterwards	66

PROLOGUE

As far back as I can remember I've been interested in human behavior. What makes a person behave in certain ways? Why do people act differently in the same situation? I'm convinced that every human being is a mixture of biology and the environment. People become who they are through a lifetime of experiences. Only recently I begin to examine the fabric of my own life. What events occurred that made me make certain life choices? As I asked myself that question, I decided that one focal point helped shape me. I realized that my experiences growing up with an autistic brother greatly impacted my life. My greatest hope is that a description of my life, as the sister of an autistic person, will provide insight to others who are struggling with the same issues. I also hope that those who do not have a handicapped family member will understand just a little better the challenges those of us who do face.

I can't remember a time in my life when there was not a sense of foreboding; —a type of nameless anxiety hanging over me like a dark shadow that I desperately tried to escape. In her book, "The Normal One," Dr. Safer puts into words how I feel. "Pessimism is the hardest, most persistent legacy...If something is even a little wrong, I assume it's rotten to the core; like a cold, a temporary setback could signal the beginning of a relentless downward spiral. This attitude doesn't interfere with my efforts, but it mars my pleasure and satisfaction and makes relaxation elusive. Curiously, I reserve negativity exclusively for myself; for everybody else, I am an enthusiastic proponent of the power to change through insight, work, and will. A paradoxical combination of exuberance, resilience, and catastrophic expectation coexist in my temperament."[1]

I chose Social Work as my profession. Even though I had low expectations for myself, I always had incredible optimism for the people I worked with who were in seemingly impossible situations. Essentially, I lived vicariously through their victories.

It gave my life meaning. Until I read the passage, I felt that my negative slant on life was a basic character flaw. I always internalized negativity, and I internalized all the bad feelings because to be angry at my brother was not acceptable. He couldn't help his disability. While that is an immutable fact, I now realize that being angry at an unfair situation is only human. Refusing to own my feelings was to deny my very humanity. The only way to remain sane is to acknowledge anger for the unfairness of disabilities.

I don't assign any blame to my parents. We lived under circumstances that never could be described as normal. Even the most empathic people could not completely understand the total

---

[1] Safer. The Normal One: Life with a Difficult or Damaged Sibling. Safer, Jeanne (pg 23)

picture. And who can blame them? I lived with autism daily but cannot tell you with complete accuracy what it was like because for me this was the reality of my existence. I did not have an alternate life in a parallel universe to compare to others. Dr. Safer expresses that "whatever the family dynamics ends up being, the normal child will be scarred, even if the scars do not show."[2]

I thought that after I married and had my own family this unnamed anxiety would magically disappear. I tried desperately to make this happen. I made a valiant effort to make everything in my life perfect. After all, this had worked for me when I lived with my brother, (or I thought it had). I don't tell a sob story, and I am not a victim. I have a wonderful husband and children. Life is good for me, but I realized only recently that I, and I alone, am responsible for taking care of my own mental health. I had unresolved anger from my childhood that caused depression in my adulthood. There I said it, and I don't regret it. Acknowledging that there is a problem is the first step in any healing process. Hello, my name is Lisa, and I am the sister of an autistic person.

---

[2] Safer. The Normal One.

1
A Rough Beginning

If you asked me to identify the exact moment in time when I realized that my brother was different, I couldn't. As far back as I can remember, my brother's autism was a part of my everyday reality. Scottie was born in March of 1967, the first child of my parents. I was born seventeen months later. My mom reports that at 10:00 a.m. on March 30, Dad took her to the hospital. At this point, she was already having hard contractions. Despite her intense contractions, the doctor reported that she was not dilating in correspondence to the level of contractions. The doctor offered her pain medicine after several hours of labor which she refused at first. The medical staff took her to have x-rays done. They wanted to be sure she could have the baby naturally. The doctor discovered that there was no amniotic fluid surrounding the baby, but he still chose not to do a C-section. After hours of painful labor, mom finally consented to have pain medicine. She was given some medicine that she was apparently allergic to. She hallucinated. These hallucinations took the form of soap opera doctors conversing with her from General Hospital and insects she described as amoeba-like in a slimy solution that seemed to be dripping from the ceiling. After almost 24 hours of painful labor, my mom gave birth to Scott, a baby she describes as horribly wrinkled and very blue. Like all infants, Scott was given the Apgar Test, and my dad reports that it was a normal score. Although Scott's birth was far from picture-perfect, my parents took home a child that seemed perfectly healthy and normal.

Since Scott seemed to develop normally, the difficult birth became a distant memory. He hit all the milestones that children should have as a developing infant. He didn't seem abnormal in any way. In fact, if anything he appeared very bright. However, 1967 was a different world than 2002. Mental illness was more of an enigma. Looking back, mom realized that some subtle signs of his autism might have been present then.

Scott always welcomed touch and as a baby, loved to be caressed and rocked. In this way, he didn't seem to be the typical autistic child. However, his attachment seemed to have extreme overtones. Attachment by children to their parents is, of course, healthy, and normal. Scott's clingy attachment was extreme. My parents could never enjoy a night out because he could never be left with anyone else. Mom states that when he was about nine months old, she and my dad planned to go to a college football game.

Mom's close friends were excited about the prospect of watching the cute chubby little boy. Mom and Dad left Scott while he was still crying but thought that he would adjust like most children and be okay in a few minutes. Scott screamed for an hour and a half despite the best efforts of their friends to quiet him. Fortunately, these friends lived just down the road from my mom's parents. In desperation, they took my brother to my grandma's. Scott 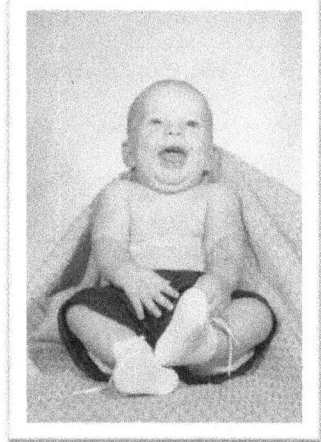 remained highly agitated but stopped crying, as long as his grandmother held him. He only completely calmed down after Mom and Dad returned from the game. Further, Mom could never leave him in a Sunday school class without his extreme crying. She always volunteered to teach his class.

In addition to over-attachment to my mom, another early sign of Scott's problem involved his hypersensitivity to noises. He was terrified of the noise produced by both the vacuum cleaner and the electric mixer. Mom said that she would have to wait until he went to sleep before she could vacuum the house.

Although the reasons for my brother's descent into a world known only to him are not completely clear, one event seems to have served as a possible precursor. Like many young couples, my parents struggled financially. Before my parents' marriage, Dad served in the military. Even though it was the height of the Vietnam War, my father felt that rejoining the army was the best course of action to provide for his wife and young children.

He was stationed in Dallas, Texas, for his first military assignment when Scott was not quite two. Changes in Scott's behavior were not extreme at this time. Mom reports that he seemed a little quieter, but otherwise, he did not have any drastic problems. However, after the next move to San Antonio, Texas, where Dad attended school to become a lab technician, signs of impending trouble began to appear. This is when another possible clue that there was a problem, although more subtle than the first two, began to concern Mom. Scott developed normally in many ways as defined by reaching developmental milestones. He sat up at six months and walked at eleven months. He began speaking single words and phrases at the correct age. At the age of three, he even spoke in sentences. Mom became a little concerned about his development when he was around the age of four because she noticed that other children his age would engage in small conversations. Despite his ability to speak in sentences, Scott rarely if ever put together several sentences in a conversational form. Mom took him to the pediatrician and voiced her concern. The doctor examined Scott and spoke with him. He reassured her that Scott was fine. Mom, of course, was relieved and filed away her fears as over-anxious first-time mom fears.

During this time, Scott began a slow withdrawal from reality. When children from the neighborhood tried to initiate play, he would simply pick up his toys and move to a different spot where he could play alone. After several rebuffed attempts to interact, children in the neighborhood gave up. Eventually, Scott's communication became almost totally non-verbal. He had his needs met by pointing at what he needed or wanted. Mom said that she was deeply concerned because Scott was not talking, but she figured that he would be fine once he started school and adjusted to his new environment. The opposite turned out to be true.

The Boy Inside

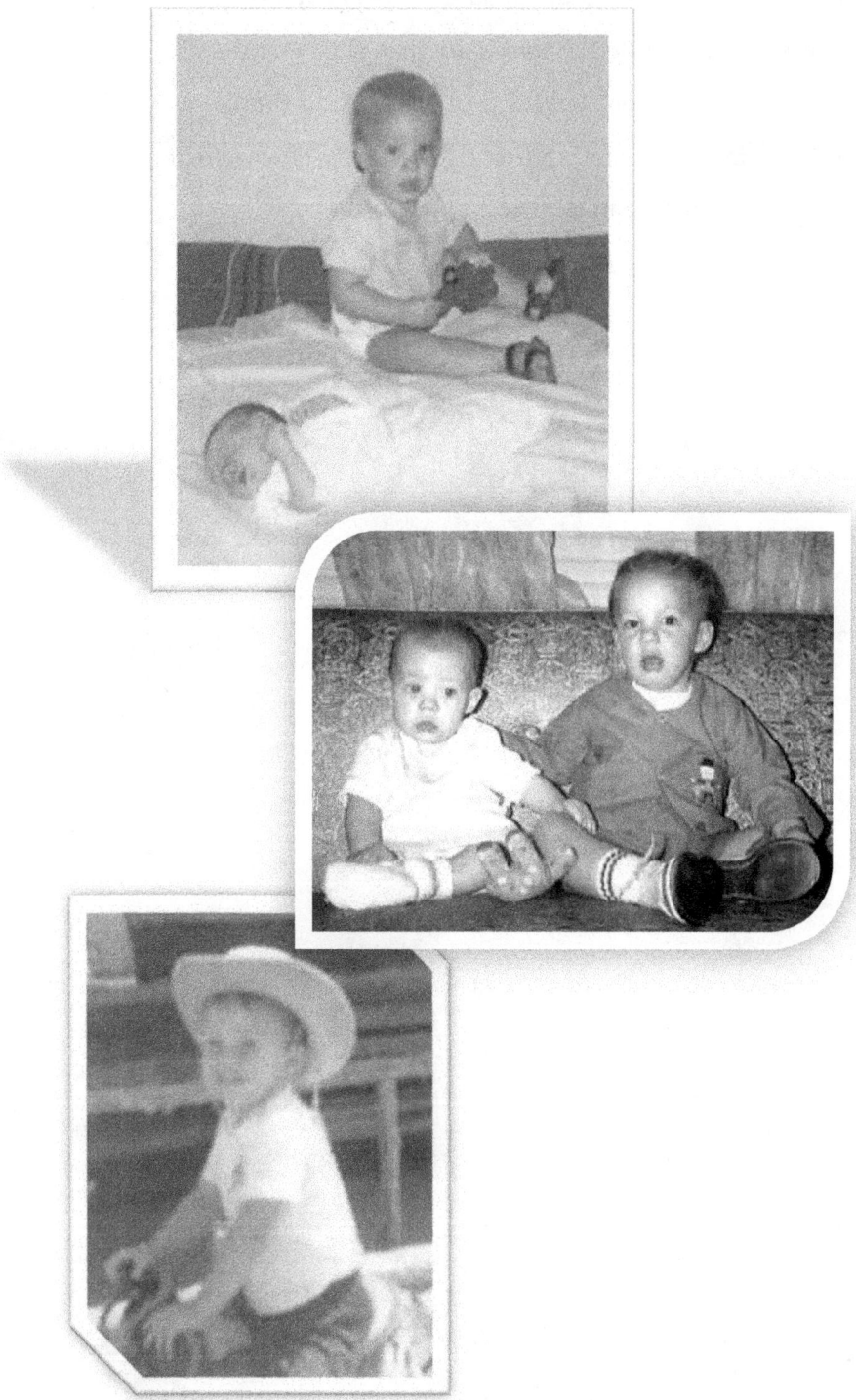

2
Kindergarten and other adventures

Probably the last straw for Scott was the combination of moving from Texas to Fort Huachuca, Arizona, and starting kindergarten. Change is difficult for many people, but it is life-shattering for people with autism. The move and starting school were apparently such drastic changes that my brother fell over the edge that he had been teetering on for some time. He descended headfirst into autism.

Scott attended classes for about three weeks. His teacher said that he was not able to stay in his seat even for a few moments, and he would not talk at all by this time. Instead of words he made noises and hummed. Mom was called in to speak with the teacher. She was told that Scott had gone berserk, running around the room ripping pictures off the wall and tearing apart pillows. She was advised to get immediate psychological testing done.

Mom was referred to the Tucson Children's Evaluation Clinic. Scott underwent a whole day of psychological tests. The doctors concluded that beyond a shadow of a doubt he was severely mentally retarded with autistic-like qualities. My mother was completely devastated. She argued with the doctor that this diagnosis could not be correct. Her son was a bright child before his mysterious withdrawal from reality. He even seemed above average. He could read simple words at age four. This just could not be right. The examiners insisted that the tests were accurate. Because of his total retreat from the world, my brother was unable to respond appropriately to questions. Therefore, his inability to answer the simplest questions led to the conclusion that he was retarded.

My mom spoke with Scott's pediatrician about the test results. She told him that the tests could not be correct. Basically, they told her that she was in denial and needed to accept the truth however painful it was. Mom went home and instructed my father to watch my brother and me. She went into her room and cried until she could not cry anymore. She continued to cry off and on for three days.

Since I was very young, I don't remember much about this time. My most vivid memory was my brother's extreme hyperactivity. He was in constant motion. He ran aimlessly, and my mother had a difficult time keeping up with him. She spent a great deal of energy just making sure he was safe. Scott continued to descend into a place where his family was unable to go. He screamed a lot and made unintelligible sounds.

He no longer welcomed touch even from Mom, to whom he used

to cling. He was nearly impossible to keep up with. Mom had to keep him within her sight, or he would be out of the house and gone before she could count to three. My parents put up a tall fence around the backyard which the fence salesman said could not be climbed. Scott climbed it. Mom would put him in his room and lock it in the hope that she could get some housework completed. Scott would remove the screen from the window and climb out. His nickname became Houdini for obvious reasons. Despite her best efforts, Scott disappeared more than once and had to be brought back by the military police.

Usually, his disappearance episodes were short-lived. However, despite my youth, I remember one day of complete agony. He disappeared one morning, causing the family terrible anxiety. When my mother realized that he was nowhere to be found, she alerted my father and the Military Police. The police searched the base while my parents frantically searched the neighborhood. Neighbors reported that they had observed Scott earlier that day. He ran through the neighborhood turning on everyone's water faucets. After this, no one had seen a trace of him. I was beginning to feel that they would never find him.

Despite his disability, I was very close to my brother since we were so near in age. I was five at that time, and I still remember the feelings of helplessness and loss of control. The world was not as certain or safe as I had once thought. I prayed to God that he would bring my brother home safely.

Scott had disappeared sometime in the early morning. It was approaching dusk. Finally, an MP car pulled up. Standing in the

driveway of our house, I squinted to see if I could catch a glimpse of my brother in the waning light. At first, I didn't see him. Oh no! I thought they still had not found him or worse yet something awful has happened to him. The closer I got to the car, however, I thought I saw a figure in the back seat. My mom had already started toward the car. The relief on my mom's face told me that they had found Scott.

As the MP opened the door to let my brother out, he began to give my mother a stern lecture. "We found your son just wandering around aimlessly." He stated something to the effect, "Miss, you need to keep a better watch on your child. You obviously are lax, or this would not have happened." My mother tried to explain my brother's problems and hyperactivity. He repeated that she must do a better job in keeping up with her child. Even as young as I was, I felt the intense sting of injustice. How dare you judge us, I thought. You don't live with Scott. The MP's left and Mom cried. So did I.

In contrast to Scott's obvious emotional problems, he was quite striking in appearance. His skin was ivory, almost like fine porcelain. His dark hair and eyes stood out even more because of his color. He was tall and lean. I was very proud of my handsome brother. His angelic looks were only his physical shell. I believed that if I could see into his soul, it would be beautiful too.

Physically, my brother was healthy. There was one exception, however. Scott had laughing and crying spells which seemed to occur spontaneously and varied in duration. A neurologist explained to my mom that these spells were caused by brain seizures. The laughing seizures didn't bother me as much as the crying ones. He would cry mournfully as if he had lost a loved one to death. It broke my heart. We just wanted to comfort him. Scott was prescribed two different medicines simultaneously. The combination helped his seizures and eventually helped with his hyperactivity.

Two peas in a pod

Boating fun

3
ITS AUTISM? WHAT A RELIEF

After I completed kindergarten in Arizona, Dad was given orders to move to Frankfurt, Germany. I was a little bit scared about going to a foreign country, but my mom told us it would be a great adventure. Scott still did not talk, and I felt very protective of him. I considered him to be vulnerable, and I had to defend him. Once we settled into life in Germany, things ran pretty smoothly.

When we first arrived, I made friends with the neighborhood kids. Naturally, Scott's wild running and muteness attracted attention. I explained that he was different but harmless and that they should not be afraid. Anytime I felt that someone was making fun of him or bothering him I quickly jumped to his defense. With great indignation and a stern voice, I would tell the person harassing him to leave him alone. Since most of the time I was two sizes smaller than the person I confronted, it probably wasn't a wise move. I had a booming voice for a small girl,

Special Olympics in Germany

and my bluffs usually worked.

Although Scott rarely if ever verbalized, his hyperactivity was curtailed to the point that it was manageable. I have always had the philosophy that if it is not broken don't fix it. A neurologist in Germany, unfortunately, had a different perspective. He said that my brother's EEG's showed some abnormality in brain waves but not enough to warrant the continuation of his medicine. He ordered the medicine to be stopped. Almost immediately my brother became unmanageably hyperactive again. My mom had to reverse the lock on the front door of our apartment to keep Scott from escaping. Despite her best efforts, Scott would escape and destroy neighbors' property. Mom reported that one of our neighbors was a sculptor and had several statues sitting on his balcony. Scott smashed all of them. The understanding man told mom what had happened. He was a little upset over his artwork being destroyed, but he told mom that he knew that something was wrong with Scott, so he was not blaming her or angry. Mom apologized and explained to this neighbor Scott's problems. She showed him the reversed doorknob in an attempt to explain what she was up against. He was one of a handful of compassionate and kind people that crossed our path. Bless him, wherever he may be.

During the time when Scott was off his medicine, mom tried hard to hold onto her sanity. At each medical review, she would tell the doctor of Scott's negative behavior change. This back and forth lasted for three or four months. Finally, mom insisted that he be placed back on the medicine. The doctor reluctantly complied. Scott's behavior began to improve within a week.

Mom says that prayer was the only refuge she had sometimes. Her friends would say, "I don't know how you do it." Mom would respond the same way each time: "I was not given a choice. This was the child I was given, and with God's help I will raise him." Even with her great determination, Mom felt weak at times and sought help from a higher power. She relates that one Mother's Day she knelt down by my brother's bed and prayed all night for his healing or the strength to raise him. God chose to give her strength.

As my mom promised, living in Germany was a great adventure. My family took full advantage of seeing the sights during the three years we lived there. Almost every Saturday, we would go Volksmarching, (walking a set course through the countryside, – usually six miles). We explored medieval castles, ancient churches, and historical sites, like Hitler's hideout located in Austria. Scott's spirit seemed to be set free during these times. He was more relaxed when we were exploring the countryside or some old castle. Scott and I didn't communicate verbally, but I felt we both enjoyed the exploration and the freedom we felt during the family outings.

Scott and I couldn't play like most siblings. He didn't interact normally. However, there were a few ways we connected. He had a complete fascination with Legos. He would build the most beautiful structures. He was like a miniature architect. He would build beautiful houses. He used different colored bricks and layered them in specific designs. He would put doors and windows in his houses and line them up in the perfect way. He would top his house with a roof that complimented the design he had chosen. When he was finished, I would sit there in awe. How did he do that? Try as I might, my buildings never matched his. Scott would never speak, but I talked to him as if he would respond.

"Scott," I would say, "that is a beautiful house." Sometimes I could get a smile. As simple as that seems, it was a way to have a relationship with him. My brother also had a fascination with hair. He liked to comb my dolls' hair. He even gave my new Christmas doll a haircut. I was not happy. Scott also liked to comb my hair and would roll my hair in foam rollers at night. I always requested that he roll my hair because it was a way to spend time with him, and he did a great job. In the morning, my hairdo looked great. I had my own hairdresser.

Through his school, Scott got involved in the Special Olympics. It was such an incredible outlet for his boundless energy. He had natural athletic ability in the sport of track. I think I enjoyed the Special Olympics probably as much as Scott. Since everybody there was disabled in some way, I felt completely comfortable and at ease. I didn't have to explain him. People just understood.

Scott would compete in all the field and track events. I watched from the stands. The gun would fire, and he would leap forward in a great lunge. He was amazingly fast and agile. Dust flew from his shoes as he gave it all he had. Mom and I cheered, "Go Scott go" until we were hoarse. Scott broke the ribbon crossing the finish line way ahead of the other competitors. I told mom I didn't think it was fair. After all, my brother had exceptional talent and the other competitors didn't have a chance.

Scott seemed to appreciate his accomplishment, especially when he was escorted to the top podium and a gold medal was placed around his neck. His expression and smiles let us know that he felt proud of his wins. By the end of the day, he would have several gold medals. He rarely came in second or third. He would wear his medals days after the Olympics were over. Finally, he would take them off and let us display them in his room.

While we were in Germany, Scott was finally correctly diagnosed. He was still attending school under the label of severely mentally retarded. It didn't take much observation for Scott's teacher in Germany to accurately name Scott's disorder. He had worked for several years in California with autistic children, and he had no doubt that this was Scott's problem. His apparent retardation was secondary to his real problem. Scott's withdrawal, rocking back and forth, hyperactivity, and strange noises suddenly made more sense when described as symptoms of a mental disorder. His inability to learn was not retardation, but rather a result of his autism.

Mom set out to learn as much as she could about her son's disorder, reading everything she could find about autism. Although this diagnosis was unofficial, it was such a relief to have the right information. He would later be officially diagnosed by a psychiatrist.

In January of 1977, my sister Julie was born. Even with my brother's disability, it never occurred to me that something could be wrong with her. I was just excited to have a new sister. She was a completely healthy, normal little girl. I learned later that my father had anxiety about her birth. Although fathers were allowed to be in the delivery room, he chose to stay in the waiting room. Mom said that he didn't know if he could handle it if something was wrong with her. The day mom brought Julie home, I was overjoyed. She looked angelic. She had beautiful dark eyes, olive skin, and coal-black hair. I couldn't tell if Scott liked the new family member. He seemed neither happy nor sad. Of course, this flat reaction was normal for Scott.

The day our sister came home.

Birthday fun with sisters

4
Advocating for an Education

In late 1977, my father received orders to go to Fort Riley, Kansas. It was always a struggle to find an appropriate school for Scott. At this time mainstreaming was not being practiced, or at least not as much as now. Scott was put into a totally inappropriate setting. My mother reluctantly agreed with placing him in this school because she felt that she had no other choice. The school was made up of severely — and I would say profoundly — retarded individuals. Many of the students were not potty trained.

My brother was the only autistic child. He was much higher functioning than all of the other students. Despite his autism, Scott was able to do most self-help skills common for his age. He bathed himself and brushed his teeth when encouraged to do so. He could dress when his clothes were laid out for him. He had very good table manners. Due to this inappropriate educational setting, he began to digress rapidly. His behavior became increasingly worse. He had outbursts of screaming and self-injury. He would beat himself in the head so hard that it scared me. It did not take a genius to figure out that this behavior started when he was placed in a classroom totally wrong for his needs.

Mom was proactive in relation to her son's education. Therefore, she attended seminars that might help her in providing the best services for my brother. By providential design, she had attended a seminar (ironically presented by a man from my parents' hometown, Jonesboro, Arkansas), that presented information about a law that had recently been passed that guaranteed all children an education appropriate to their particular needs.

Mom filed her notes away and essentially forgot about them. As Scott's behavior reached a critical point, she knew that it was time to advocate for the best interest of her child. Scott's school was way out in the country in a building that the school district had deemed not acceptable for normal students. She scheduled a meeting with the school superintendent.

He was uncooperative and condescending. He told her that nothing could be done. He told her she might as well accept that Scott's current school was the best she could expect. The superintendent had not counted on two things, however. Mom doesn't give up easily, and she had prayed before she talked with him. She told me later what had happened at the meeting. After the superintendent said that nothing could be done, Mom silently prayed for wisdom from the Lord. Almost immediately she remembered the information presented at the seminar that guaranteed each child an appropriate education. She began reciting information that she had learned from the class. She stated that her son was not receiving an appropriate education. She told him that if he didn't provide Scott an education that benefited him, he would be breaking the law. My brother was transferred to a better school soon after this conversation.

Baby shower

5
Scott's Place

It was also during our time in Kansas that Scott was re-evaluated by a psychiatrist. The results were not different than before except that an official diagnosis of autism was made by a qualified psychiatrist. My parents were called in to review the results. The psychiatrist was bleak about Scott's test. He shocked my parents by suggesting that they institutionalize him.

My dad asked, "Why now? He is ten years old and has lived with us all this time." He also asked if putting him in an institution would help him. In other words, could they help him get better.

"Well, no, he won't get better," the psychiatrist responded. "But it would be better for the rest of your family."

My dad said, "Thanks, but no thanks. If it does not benefit him, then it does not benefit us." My mom told me years later of my dad's decision. In the late 1970s, there was not as much community support for parents who chose to raise their disabled children at home. His commitment and love for Scott showed great courage and strength of character.

Scott rarely spoke, so it was a treat to hear him say anything. It was especially touching to hear him speak when you knew what he said was appropriate to what was happening at that particular moment. My brother liked to stand on a chair in the kitchen and watch my mother prepare supper on a regular basis. He seemed mesmerized by the cooking process.

One Saturday evening, Scott stood in his usual spot as mom fried catfish and made hush puppies. "Well, Scott, do you think this is enough hush puppies?" Scott did not respond. "Maybe I should make some more," Mom said.

As Mom stirred all the ingredients she was shocked by Scott's interruption. "You forgot the salt," Scott said.

A little stunned by Scott's rare proclamation, she regained composure. "What did you say?" Scott repeated. "You forgot the salt."

Mom thought for a moment, and then said, "You are right, Scott, I did forget the salt." Scott had observed her prepare the first batch and recognized her error. More importantly, he was able to verbalize to her what he had observed. Mom hugged Scott and praised him for his keen observation and for saving the hush puppies. This incident may seem trivial to families without disabled members, but to us, we couldn't have been more proud than if he had won a Nobel Peace Prize.

When I was around the age of ten, I remember having feelings of ambiguity. I wondered in the back of my mind if I could have a disability. After all, my brother was disabled. I knew I wasn't autistic but maybe I had some other disability. I never shared these feelings with my parents, but like most moms, my mother had keen intuition. She encouraged me in my studies and supported all my ideas, even the silly ones. I also remember her sitting down with me and asking me directly about my fears. I shared with her that I was sometimes scared — that because of Scott's problems, something might be wrong with me. She reassured me that I was a perfectly normal, intelligent little girl. Mom was very good at persuasion, and her talk helped put my fears to rest. Our conversation ended with a warm hug.

6
Germany Again

My dad was again given new orders by the Army, but this time there was a twist. Dad was, to our surprise, reassigned to Germany. Since my brother's education had not been the best in Germany, my parents made the difficult decision to separate the family for two years. My father decided to go to Germany and serve his duty while my mother, sister, brother, and I were moved to Aurora, Colorado, a suburb of Denver, to allow my brother to receive what was considered one of the best educations for autistic people at that time. My brother was talking now, but unfortunately, he only mimicked others. If Mom said, "Scott, do you want to eat?" he would repeat, "Scott, do you want to eat?" He also repeated commercials word -for- word, including using exact voice tones used by the actor in the commercial. This could be quite entertaining at times but rather annoying in public. My parents shopped for a mobile home for us to live in while Dad lived in Germany. My brother, sister, and I, of course, went along. The salesman happily showed us a variety of homes. Scott ran in and out of the trailers humming and holding his ears. Periodically, he would pause to recite a popular commercial of that time. Mom and Dad seemed unaffected by Scott's activities. They were too busy trying to secure shelter. I, on the other hand, wanted to crawl under the nearest rock. I must admit that the salesman's expressions were funny. He tried his best to pretend that Scott's behavior was not odd. After all, he wanted to make a sale.

Dad helped us settle into our new home. The day came when we would have to take Dad to Stapleton Airport for his flight to Germany. We arrived early so that we could get our last hugs and kisses. We knew they would have to last for a very long time. I'm sure Scott didn't completely understand what was happening. When Dad heard the final boarding call, he hugged all of us and cried. He grabbed his carry-on

luggage and started through the tunnel that connects the airport to the plane. The door was closed after the last passenger boarded. We ran to the window to watch Dad's plane take off. The plane taxied down the runway. I watched as his plane ascended and finally disappeared completely from sight. I felt very sad that day. It was difficult to know what my brother thought of Dad's departure. However, anytime Scott saw a plane he would say, "Dad." I guess he thought Dad flew around in a plane for two years. After all, that was the last place he had seen him.

The family in Kansas

7
"Why Me?"

Introducing Scott to the neighbors was always difficult. I was very outgoing and made friends quite easily. I decided that I should introduce myself to some kids who were sitting on their porches.

"Hi," I began. "My name is Lisa. My family just moved into the neighborhood." The kids in turn introduced themselves. We talked casually for a few minutes. Suddenly, I heard the screen door of our trailer burst open and saw my brother leap out of the house.

"Oh no," I thought, trying desperately to formulate an explanation of Scott in my mind. Scott streaked by like a lighting flash, cupping his ears with his hands and humming loudly. The neighbor kids looked shocked and even a little scared. Still not sure what to say, I just started talking.

"That's my brother, Scott. He's autistic."

"What did you say?" asked one of the kids. "He's artistic?"

"No, I said autistic. That means he's brain-damaged. He lives in his own world and cannot communicate like us. Don't worry, he won't hurt you." This explanation seemed to satisfy them, and we continued to talk.

I must confess that I didn't always handle introductions of my brother so gracefully. On our first Sunday in Aurora, Mom looked up the address of the nearest Nazarene Church and we attended. We had just sent my father off for two years. We were in a new city, and I would have to attend a new school and church. I was feeling a bit overwhelmed.

I sat in the car immobilized by fear. Once again, I would have to introduce and explain my brother to a new group of people. I wanted to scream, "Why me, God?" Mother asked me if I cared to let Scott go with me to class. I wanted to protest but I felt that this was the right thing to do. After all, Mom had all she could handle. She was single-parenting three children, one of which was severely mentally handicapped. As we entered the small church, some nice church members directed Scott and me to a classroom filled with about ten students. The young twenty-something teacher welcomed us to class. I silently prayed that Scott would act "normal" just until class was over.

For the first fifteen minutes or so everything ran smoothly. True to form, however, Scott began to squirm in his chair. I wanted to run out of the room, but it felt like my legs were paralyzed. Several strange noises burst out from Scott. He grabbed his ears and continued to hum. I couldn't even look up for some time. Finally, I said quietly to a very stunned and frightened group of children. "He's autistic."

The teacher, who was herself trying to regain composure said, "Oh, well, Lisa, could you explain to us what that is?"

I wanted to say, "I'm eleven years old, and I've lived with him all my life, but I still don't know how to explain autism." Instead, I burst into tears. The Sunday School teacher retrieved my mother from her class. Mom talked to me for a while. I don't remember what she said, except, "Do you want to skip church and go home?" I was so upset that I could only nod. I cried all the way home and said how unfair it was that I had to explain my brother. I got to admit honestly that I was angry.

Before moving to Aurora, I don't remember having a problem bringing friends home to play. As a pre-teen, this began to change. My peers' image of me suddenly became much more important. I didn't know if I wanted people from school to know about Scott. I thought that I might be shunned if they knew about my brother's disability. I felt guilty for these feelings, but I wasn't willing to take the risk of rejection by my peer group. I rarely invited my classmates to my home. I would make up excuses of why they couldn't come. I had many friends from the neighborhood and from school, but only my closest friends were allowed into my home. The fewer people who came to my house, I reasoned, the fewer explanations were necessary. In addition, the potential for embarrassing incidents would be reduced. I believe that this theory of mine stunted my social development and isolated me more than was necessary. As an eleven-year-old, I closed myself off from many wonderful experiences, but at that time I felt I must protect myself. Right or wrong, it was as important as physical survival to me at this time in my life.

The main reason we moved to Aurora was to allow my brother to receive a top-notch education. This is exactly what happened. Scott made wonderful progress. He began to communicate better. His speech had been mostly echolalia before he began this school. Now he was able to tell us what he wanted and mimicked conversation much less. I was able to go to his school on a few occasions during the open house. The facility looked new, and the school seemed well-supplied. The teachers were young, creative, and energetic. I didn't enjoy moving or the time of separation from my father but seeing my brother's progress did help ease the loneliness some. Scott's progress was worth the sacrifice.

During my father's absence, Mom sold Avon which provided an extra income and gave her a social outlet. When Scott and I were out of school for the summer, I was responsible for watching my brother and three-year-old sister. I was only eleven when I started doing this. As I look back, I now realize that caring for them was likely a lot of responsibility for an eleven-year-old. My mom checked in on us frequently during the day because she sold Avon in our mobile home park. I don't remember feeling overwhelmed by this task. Scott's behavior was relatively mild, and he really didn't give me any problems. He usually complied with my requests. He did have one behavior on which I had to keep a close eye. He would purposely try to burn himself by holding his hand on light bulbs. Scott always tried new ways to hurt himself, but his favorite at this time was burning himself. Mom would have to run his bath water to keep him from scalding himself in the water.

Halfway through Dad's year of absence from the family, he was able to come home for a visit. I was beside myself with excitement. My dad was coming home. At the airport, we waited by the door where he would emerge from the plane. I paced nervously, watching a stream of passengers file off the plane. It seemed to take an eternity. Just when I thought we might have the wrong terminal, he walked through the door. I had a lump in my throat.

"Dad!" I yelled. The entire family ran to greet him. Somehow, we all managed to hug him at the same time, including Scott. We took full advantage of Dad's one-month visit. We went on family picnics and mountain climbing in the majestic Rockies. I knew he would have to return to Germany, but I just wanted to enjoy his visit.

Then the day came when he had to leave. We took him to the airport and sent him off for one more year. Although this was difficult, our family was comforted by the fact that the next time he came home it would be for keeps.

Scott loved church

8
REUNITED

After dad served his two-year tour of Germany, he was given orders for Fort Carson, Colorado. We were living in Aurora which is about 90 miles from this army base. For about a year after his return, Dad drove back and forth from our home in Aurora to his work in Fort Carson. The long drive was taking its toll on him, not to mention the high cost of fuel. During the work week, he stayed overnight. My parents felt that moving to Colorado Springs would be the best idea. They found a lot to rent in a mobile home park about ten minutes from the army base. It was a location with incredibly lovely scenery. Mountains surrounded us. In fact, I could look out the kitchen window and see N.O.R.A.D, the mountain with all the nuclear weapons.

Although I had accepted my brother's disorder, certain events throughout life would again cause me to grieve over the person he might have been. I know mom had similar experiences. Scott had grown to be a very attractive young teenager. As was our usual pattern, we begin attending a Nazarene Church in our new city. The first Sunday at the new church I searched for my class.

As I was looking for the right classroom, Mom said, "Look Lisa." Standing outside a classroom were some cute teenage girls. Scott's behavior was normal at this particular moment. To my surprise, the girls seemed to be checking out the new cute boy, my brother.

I whispered to mom. "They're checking out Scott."

"Yes," she said. "I think they like what they see." Mom looked a little sad. She and I agreed that normally Scott would have a girlfriend at this age. Just when you think you have accepted what is, you are slapped in the face with what might have been if your loved one had been born normal.

Scott and I started new schools. I began the eighth grade. Scott was 15 years old, and he continued to go to special schools. All indications were that this school was positive for Scott. His verbal skills progressed to the point he would initiate conversation sometimes on his own. My parents were very good about treating all their children fairly. Due to Scott's special needs, however, his needs would take precedence over mine and Julie's. As I look back from an adult perspective, I realize that I was sometimes resentful of Scott's taking more of my parents' time than I felt was fair. I understood his condition intellectually, but, I wished that our family didn't revolve around his many needs. I knew that my parents put great emphasis on education. Whether imagined or not, I felt that they counted on me to succeed academically because Scott could not.

In my eighth-grade year, I worked extremely hard in school. I set a goal to get excellent grades. I studied almost obsessively. My hard work paid off with mostly A's and some B's. The next year I worked even harder, and I received straight A's on my report card the entire year. I had a deep need to prove myself and make my parents proud. I wanted to be the good kid and not cause any trouble. At the end of my ninth-grade year, I received several awards for academic excellence. My parents attended the ceremony and watched me receive these awards. After the assembly, we posed for a picture together. I had my parents' undivided attention. I felt wonderful.

Living with Scott was not always a downer. He could be quite comical at times. My dad enjoyed fishing as a hobby, and Scott would often go with him. Dad relates a humorous story about a fishing trip to the Platte River with Scott. Scott was in the river swimming while Dad cast his rod into the water. Scott always had an uncanny ability to hold his breath underwater for long periods of time. Just when we thought we would have to dive in and rescue him, he would burst through the water and gleefully shout at the top of his lungs. Another fisherman was fly fishing upstream. Scott submerged himself and Dad watched. He was under so long that Dad thought he might have to go after him. Just then, Scott popped to the surface with a great shout only a few feet from the other fisherman. Dad was afraid the man was going to have a heart attack. He left the river very quickly. My dad's sense of humor has always been keen. He likes to end this story by saying that the fisherman probably left to go home and change his underwear.

Proving that Scott was his father's son, he displayed a sense of humor on occasion despite his disabilities. Unfortunately for Julie and me, Scott's humor manifested itself in the form of teasing. The relationship between my brother and sister developed as she grew older. Scott is ten years older than Julie. Julie discovered that Scott was a great asset to getting what she wanted but couldn't reach. Scott was very cooperative and didn't understand that some things were put out of Julie's reach for a reason. She would say, "Scott, get me that," and he would comply.

When mom caught on to Julie's tactic, she told Scott to let her know when Julie made these requests. Scott would say, "Mom, Julie is bothering me." Julie learned that Scott wouldn't be her partner in crime anymore. But then, something we did not expect happened. Scott showed signs of being a normal brother. Namely, he teased Julie.

Scott would say that Julie was bothering him when she wasn't near him. He would holler from his room. "Mom, Julie is bothering me." Mom would go to Scott's room and find him sitting on his bed with a smile that looked like a cat that had just swallowed the canary. Julie would complain about being falsely accused. Mom could only laugh and say, "If he were normal, you would get much more teasing. That's what brothers do"

9
Graduation

In my tenth-grade year, I started at Fountain/Fort Carson High school. I continued to do well in school, and Scott flourished at his school. His special school made arrangements with my high school to have an integrated graduation ceremony. All the students from my brother's school who would normally graduate if they were able to attend regular high school were invited to the graduation ceremony in May of 1985. Scott, along with several of his classmates, was fitted for a cap and gown.

The day of graduation arrived. I was a little apprehensive because I was not sure how smoothly things would run. My family dressed in our Sunday best. Scott looked extraordinarily handsome. His royal blue cap and gown really looked fantastic on him. He seemed to understand what was going on. He was almost giddy. We took our seats in the bleachers of the school gym as Scott was escorted to his seat in the graduating line. My mind wandered back through the years. So many things had happened to bring Scott to this point. I never would have believed that the little hyperactive boy that had destroyed his classroom on the first day of kindergarten would soon be walking across a stage to receive his diploma. The many years of moves and constant struggles to provide Scott with the best education were about to merge in one event. My thoughts were interrupted by the beginning of the ceremony. The opening prayer was offered. The usual speeches were given. I watched Scott closely. I wondered if he could stay still for all the diplomas to be given out. Finally, Scott's row was called up to stand near the stage. A lump formed in my throat. "Scott Pieri," the principal announced. Scott climbed the stairs, and with the biggest smile I've probably ever seen on his face he grabbed the diploma with both hands. We cheered and clapped. Mom snapped a bunch of pictures. After the ceremony, the whole family posed for more photos. We wanted to remember this great day forever.

The Boy Inside

10

The Nightmare Begins

Living with my brother was always challenging, but most of the time, manageable. It never occurred to me that Scott's behavior would spiral so out of control that he could no longer live at home. After my father retired from the military, we moved back to my parent's hometown. I was 16 years old, and my brother was 18. I, of course, started attending a new high school and my brother went to an adult education program for disabled people. Scott did well in this special program. His teacher, Mark, had a gift for working with the disabled that I have rarely encountered. He somehow was able to communicate with and bring out the best in Scott. I, on a few occasions, was able to observe Scott interact with this teacher. It was obvious that Scott adored him. Scott flourished as long as he attended school. He seemed to be more adept at communicating his needs and wants. I even felt a small glimmer of hope for his future. I knew he would never be completely normal, but I thought at least he could function in a controlled home and work environment.

Scott had developed the ability to cook simple foods. He really liked to eat, and I guess he wanted to learn to cook so that he wouldn't always have to depend on his family to prepare him a snack. He learned mostly vicariously by watching Mom and me cook. His favorite snack was Ramen Noodles. He would boil the water and add the noodles without assistance. He would then add the seasoning packet. Approximately two minutes later he would consume the fruits of his labor.

I would say that the time right after we moved back to Arkansas and the following year were the most peaceful times that my family experienced with Scott as a family member. It was during this time that I experienced an unusual event. I can remember very few times that I got to see a vision of my real brother. He was so deeply hidden inside his own mind most of the time, that a glimpse of the normal him would thrill me.

When these events happened, I wanted to grab the inner Scott and snatch him into the world of reality. I wanted to scream, "Stay here." I took care of my brother in the afternoons before my mom and dad got off work. I generally kept the TV on while I did my assigned chores. I had a habit of watching the show "Love Connection" which came on at 4:00 p.m. That afternoon I, for whatever reason, had not turned on the television.

My brother was quietly sitting on the couch as I plugged in the vacuum cleaner. I was jolted out of my thoughts by a very unexpected question. "Are you going to watch the *Love Connection*?" I looked at my brother in disbelief. Still stunned, I noticed the time on the clock was straight up 4:00 p.m. Scott had observed my daily ritual and came out of himself long enough to make a logical request. In that brief moment, I almost felt that I could reach in and snatch the real Scott.

"You want to watch the *Love Connection*?" I asked.

"Yes," was his simple but appropriate response. I turned on the TV and sat down next to him. The housework could wait.

The peace was about to end. It seems that this peaceful time was only the lull before the great storm. I graduated from Jonesboro High School in 1987. I debated about going to college, so I worked a year before enrolling. Unfortunately, 1987 also marked the beginning of two tragedies for my family. Although I can't directly link these sad events to the decline of my brother, I believe that they played a role in his downward spiral.

The phone rang at our house early one Monday on a November evening. My dad answered. I heard him say, "His plane has not arrived?" Dad started to choke up. I was afraid that he was talking about my mom's brother, Jesse. He had visited at grandmother's house the day before. Most of the family was there. He lived in Texas and flew his small plane back and forth to Arkansas to visit family. When Dad got off the phone I asked, "Dad, what's going on?"

Hesitantly he answered. "Your uncle Jesse's plane is missing."

"Oh, no! It can't be," I said. We all stayed at grandma's waiting for word on the search. We waited and prayed for a week. Grandma's phone rang. They had found his plane, and there were no survivors. The family's worst fears had been realized. During this ordeal, Scott stayed mostly with Dad because he would not have understood. My uncle's funeral was the day before Thanksgiving. My mom grieved like any person who had just lost her brother in a sudden tragic accident. We did not tell Scott because we didn't think he would comprehend the concept of death. But I'm sure he sensed the spirit of grief in the family.

My grandparents naturally took the death of their son hard. My mom's dad had always been a jovial soul. When he laughed, it started in his belly and worked its way up until it burst forth. He was still a happy person, but he never was the same as before his son's death. Grandpa Sellars and Scott got along famously. My grandma and grandpa watched Scott when my mom needed them to. I can't say that Grandpa understood my brother, but he accepted him with love. Scott always wanted to follow him outside and watch him work in the garden or feed the animals. They seemed to have an unspoken language that only they understood.

In January of 1989, my grandpa Sellars fell ill. At first, he thought it was just a bad case of pneumonia, but he couldn't seem to shake it. After a month of being sick, he decided to go to the doctor. The X-rays showed a tumor in his lungs. It turned out to be lung cancer. Mom and her siblings spent many hours helping my grandma with Grandpa. Mom was limited in how much time she could help because it would throw Scott into a tailspin if she were gone too long. On August 18, 1989, Grandpa lost his battle with cancer. Scott stayed with friends while we attended the funeral. My mom didn't know how to explain why Grandpa would no longer be at my grandparents' house. She thought that saying nothing would be best unless Scott brought up the subject.

Scott still stayed with Grandma sometimes, and she noticed that he seemed more restless than usual. He walked from room to room in the house. He didn't say anything. After he repeated this pattern about three times, Grandma said, "Scott, what do you want?" Scott did not respond but continued wandering from room to room.

Finally, Grandma said, "Are you looking for Grandpa, Scottie?"

"Yes," Scott said.

"Scott," Grandma said, "come and sit down with me on the sofa." Scott complied with her request. "Grandpa went to heaven to be with Jesus. I know you miss him." Scott seemed to understand. He stopped wandering. He never asked about Grandpa again.

11
The Nightmare Continues

The events that followed in the next two years could only be described as a nightmare, a nightmare from which I would never awake. I was attending the local university in my town and living at home. My brother was neither attending school nor working. He seemed lost. Scott's personality could be described as generally mild, although he still had periods of self-mutilating. His personality went through a rapid transformation. He would scream at the top of his lungs and beat himself in the head with his fist. These fits would have a sudden onset with no apparent reason. It was extremely unnerving, to say the least. The number of episodes would vary from day to day, but usually, there was at least one fit per day. My parents had to hold his hands to keep him from badly injuring himself. As a consequence, my mom and dad would be injured. My brother is extremely strong. His behavior progressed to the point that he not only accidentally hurt us but began lashing out at family members. Without warning, he would repeatedly hit us. For reasons we don't understand, my mother seemed especially targeted by him. He left bruises on at least one occasion, but my mother did not tell me about the bruises until much later. These fits also would occur at night. I remember one incident in particular. I was awakened at three a.m. as I heard what can only be described as a horror film scream come from my brother's room. I jumped to my feet and ran into his room. My parents joined me soon after. I don't know what caused this or any other of his outburst. He was beating his head with his fist leaving a very large red mark on his forehead. It seemed like an eternity before we could calm him down. He was on enough behavioral medication to sedate a horse. Scott's medicine was changed frequently with no visible improvement.

I can honestly say that Scott's behavior made me scared of him for the first time in my life. He was demonstrating behavior that we had never seen before. One Sunday

afternoon, my family visited with my Grandmother Sellars. Scott was especially agitated on this day. He sat right next to Mom on the sofa. From across the room, I observed him grimacing and clasping his hands tightly together. My mom tried to calm him by speaking in a soft voice and patting his hands gently. This tactic was to no avail. Scott popped up and humming loudly, ran out the front door. I checked to see where he went by looking out the front window. He was running wildly in Grandma's yard. Since the yard was fenced, Mom thought that it might be good for him to run off some energy. Some of my uncles were out in the yard playing horseshoes. One of them came in to report that Scott was in the process of demolishing a cable spool with a sledgehammer. Some of my younger cousins were playing in the yard, and I was scared for their safety. Mom retrieved Scott from the yard, and we went home soon after that.

Self-injury and violence toward family members were hard to deal with daily. More difficult than this, however, was Scott's "other" inappropriate behavior. Again, without any apparent cause, my brother would expose himself in public. This would usually happen after he used the restroom. He would walk out with his pants around his ankles. We would guard against this behavior by standing right in front of the bathroom and making sure he was appropriately dressed before letting him come out. This, unfortunately, was not the only outlet for Scott's newfound exhibitionism. On several occasions, he decided to walk out the back door of our home completely in the buff. Fortunately, these few incidents would be in the early morning hours. If our neighbors ever saw him, we never were told. We became aware of Scott's activities because mom couldn't find him anywhere in the house one morning. As she began to search our neighborhood, she thought she saw someone way down the sidewalk but at that point, she could not tell. When she got closer, she realized that it was indeed Scott and to her shock and horror he was in his birthday suit. She ran to him and escorted him into the house.

When my mom related what had happened, I was mortified. "Why on earth would he do this? I hope the neighbors didn't see him. How much more are we supposed to bear?" My thoughts ran wild. My nerves were completely blown. If someone said boo, I would jump ten feet in the air. Scott's behavior grew steadily worse with each passing

week. Episodes of screaming became more and more frequent. To be honest I tried to avoid being in public with Scott, especially as his behavior became more unpredictable. I was embarrassed.

The simplest trip to town became an ordeal if Scott came with us. Mom, my sister Julie, and I went to the mall one afternoon to shop. I begged my mom to leave Scott with my dad. She felt that he would do all right and insisted on taking him. It was a hot summer day, and we had just walked into the first store. As my mom stood looking at clothes, I noticed the increasing agitation on my brother's face.

"Julie," I whispered, "he's fixing to blow a gasket, right here in this crowded store." "Yeah, I know," she said. "Mom, maybe we ought to go. Scott seems upset." "I think he will be okay," Mom responded.

I leaned over again to my sister. "You do what you want, but I'm going to be at the other side of this store when he explodes." Approximately a minute after we reached the other side of the store, I heard a series of screams. I looked at my sister, and she looked at me. My sister in typical Julie form said, "Well. I didn't see that coming, did you?"

"No," I said. "Never would have guessed that."

12

Nowhere to Turn

Each day seemed to get worse. It is such a helpless feeling to see someone you love fall to pieces before your very eyes. There are no adequate words for this kind of pain. Love just does not seem to be enough. Scott's violence increased so much that there did not seem to be a break day or night. As a family, we were all completely exhausted. My mother was never one to give up easily, but even she realized that we needed outside help. We were not sure what to do. Desperation set in one Saturday, and Mom started looking in the phone book. She called the local Community Mental Health system, and they told her to bring him in for an assessment. I felt some relief. Finally, we might get assistance. To my shock, Mom returned a couple of hours later with my brother.

"Mom, what happened?" I asked. The Community Mental Health Center had conducted an assessment and determined that Scott did not meet the criteria for admission. They had asked my brother if he was suicidal or if he heard voices. They also asked if my brother appeared homicidal.

"He's autistic," my mom explained. Scott, of course, was not able to answer these questions in an intelligible manner. They suggested that my mom call the helpline. The helpline suggested that she call the Mental Health Center.

"I already tried that," she exclaimed. We seemed to be traveling in circles. Even though Mom was not one to cry, she seemed close to tears. "Please tell me what I can do. We need help."

I have always been a crier. I was physically and mentally spent. I sobbed uncontrollably. I vowed in my heart at that very moment to help others in crisis. I never wanted another family to feel so helpless.

A few days later, my brother reached another critical behavioral state. Mom was so desperate that she took him to the local ER. She explained to the ER secretary about his violence.

Yes, ma'am," the lady said. "Take a seat, and you will be called back as soon as possible." Mom took a seat reluctantly, praying that Scott would not hurt anyone in the ER. At this point, she didn't know what he might do. Scott paced the floor in a highly agitated state. Later, Mom said that she thought he was going to blow any minute She went to speak with the ER attendant again.

"When do you think we can be seen? I worry that my son will become violent and hurt someone."

Now, somewhat annoyed, the ER lady repeated that mom would have to wait her turn. No sooner had she uttered the words than my brother began swinging his arms in a wild windmill style. He struck Mom in the face and chest. Blood came from her forehead and dripped onto the floor. Needless to say, the ER staffers were stunned.

Sarcastically, Mom said, "Well, are you going to help me now or shall I continue to stand here and bleed?"

After the initial shock wore off, the attendant said, "Oh yes ma'am. I'll call security." The staff provided her with a towel to apply pressure to her face. Quickly the security took my brother to a lockup room for mental health patients. Scott was seen by a psychiatrist the next day. He suggested that Scott be institutionalized.

A social worker from Developmental Disability Services worked with the hospital to find a placement for my brother at a Human Development Center. We had an HDC in our town, but there was a two-year waiting list. My brother was in the hospital lockup room for about three weeks. He filled his days by watching TV and continuously adjusting his bed's head and foot controls. He often looked like a sandwich lodged in the center of the bed with the head and foot sticking straight in the air forming a U-shape.

I visited him several times. It is difficult to admit that I felt a sense of relief. Peace was restored at our home. I tried to hide the terrible guilt I felt. My sister and I talked about our feelings, and we agreed we couldn't show them in front of Mom. I felt so conflicted inside. I didn't want Scott to be institutionalized, but I knew that his living at home was not an option anymore. We had done all we could do humanly to keep my brother at home. How do you give up on a family member? It's worse than death. They are still alive, but you are powerless to help them. Mental illness swallows them up before your eyes and you stand and watch.

13

Institutionalization

After the three-week period, word came from the social worker that a spot had been found at an HDC near Little Rock, AR. This institution was approximately 130 miles from our hometown. The day came to transport Scott, who was now 23 years old. Mom, the social worker, and Scott made the two and a half-hour trip to deliver him to his new home. Mom returned home and didn't say much about the trip. I'm sure it was too painful.

It was a few months before I was able to visit Scott because of the long distance. I dreaded the visit. I had never been to an institution. The reality set in, and I didn't know if I could handle it. As we pulled up to the three-story structure, I swallowed hard and mentally tried to prepare myself for the visit. We entered the front door and asked the receptionist where Scott could be found.

"He is on the second floor," she stated. We were greeted by some of the residents as we searched for the elevator. Mom and I walked down a long, dark hall. We finally located Scott's room. As we entered the room, I was struck by the bleakness. The white walls were bare. An old dark wooden dresser was the only furniture on Scott's side of the room except for his cot-like bed. He was sitting on his bed with his head hanging.

"Scott, it's Mom and Lisa," Mom said. He lifted his head and bounced toward us. He seemed glad to see familiar faces.

I hugged him. "Scott, I miss you."

"Miss me," he repeated.

"Yes, Scott, I love and miss you very much." Emotion flooded my body. I found it difficult to catch my breath. Scott's roommate came over to talk to us. He had Downs Syndrome, and he looked to be about the same age as my brother. He was very talkative, so we decided to leave the room and tour the facility to get some personal time with Scott. Mom bought Scott his favorite candy and soda from a vending machine. We visited him for a couple of hours. Visiting Scott for the first time at the HDC slapped me in the face with reality. This was now his home. It was a different outcome than I had dreamed for my brother's life.

When the time came for us to leave, I could tell Scott didn't want us to go. The sadness on his face when we told him we were going is still etched into my memory. We left him at the front entrance promising to return soon. I knew the pain Mom felt so I fought back tears with such intensity I thought my head would explode. Silently, she started the car. We drove around the building. Suddenly, the car came to a sudden stop.

Mom pointed to a second-story window and exclaimed, "Look, Lisa." I strained my eyes for a moment trying to focus on what she was pointing at. Scott's angelic face and the palms of his hands were smashed against the window. He had gone to the other side of the institution to watch us leave. My heart was completely broken.

"Mom," I said, "he wants to go home with us." The pain in Mom's eyes made it useless to fight back the tears anymore. Mom began to cry, and we drove away. "Mom," I finally said. "Tell me how this is fair? We tried so hard to keep him with us."

"It's not fair, Lisa," Mom said. "Some things in life just are not fair." We talked and cried all the way home.

14
After Effects

At the time of Scott's institutionalization, I was a junior in college trying to get a degree in Social Work. Choices in life, I believe, are influenced by life experiences. I needed to help others because I was not able to help my brother. Maybe I could help families in crisis because my family had been through a crisis. I continued to visit my brother as often as possible. He also visited home on special occasions, like holidays and his birthday. His behavior was still violent at times but steadily became calmer.

I finished my degree in December of 1992. Prior to graduation, I work twenty hours a week for a program that provided community services to the disabled. I continued to work for this program after graduation. In January of the following year, I met the man of my dreams on a blind date. I knew Kendal had a heart of gold just by our conversations.

We have been together since our third date. When we began to talk about marriage, I thought I should mention my brother. I was not completely certain how he would react, but I knew any man I married would have to like Scott. Kendal, like many people, had not heard of autism. I explained all the behaviors as best as I could. After I finished my description, I waited for his response.

"He sounds interesting," he said. "I can't wait to meet him."

Delighted by his response, I said, "He will be home for a visit in July. I will introduce you then."

The weekend of the Fourth of July my brother came for his visit. My mom and dad had promised to take Scott on a camping trip. I never enjoyed camping as much as the rest of the family, but I thought it would be a good chance to visit Scott and introduce him to my future husband. Kendal loves to camp, and he thought this sounded like a great idea. We met my parents and Scott at the State Park near our home. They had already set up camp the night before. Kendal greeted my parents as Scott stood behind them.

"Kendal," I said, "this is my brother Scott. Scott, this is Lisa's boyfriend Kendal."

"Kendaaaal," he repeated.

"Nice to meet you, Scott."

"Nice to meet me," Scott responded. Kendal extended his hand to shake Scott's hand, which Scott was more than happy to do. Scott gripped his hand so hard and for so long that Kendal probably wondered if he would ever get his hand back. Since it was approaching dark when we arrived, Kendal put up his pup tent. Kendal and I stayed up late sitting by the campfire, talking about many things including my brother.

Around midnight, Kendal went to his tent, and I slept in the back seat of Mom and Dad's car. I hate tents. The next day we all ate breakfast, and Scott ran around wildly, scaring the other campers. We kept a good eye on Scott, but later in the day, he disappeared. Mom asked Kendal if he would check in the men's bathroom for Scott.

Before Kendal was able to go inside the bathroom, he heard Scott. "HAAAH HAAAH." Kendal couldn't help but laugh.

"Hey Scott" he yelled "are you in there?" Again, Scott responded with HAAAH HAAAH.

"Come on out Scott, your mother is looking for you." My brother came bouncing out of the bathroom still laughing. He ran back to camp. As Kendal told us what had happened, he was near tears from laughing. I thought if he accepts my brother, then he must be a wonderful man. I, of course, already thought that he was a kind soul, but this incident confirmed to me his true heart.

Kendal and I married on August 27, 1993, in a small, nice wedding. My sister served as my maid of honor. My brother did not attend because his behavior still would not allow it. I had another "special" guest, however, attend that happy day. Joe was a mentally retarded, schizophrenic man that I had worked with for almost two years. Two of his case managers and friends brought him to our wedding (with my invitation of course). Everything in the ceremony went as planned. I was told later that one incident happened.

Apparently, when my dad was walking me down the aisle, Joe said, loudly enough that the people in the back rows heard him, "They look like a penguin and a peacock." I was glad Joe was there to entertain. I wished my brother could have understood my special day and shared in my joy.

I turned twenty-five about a week after our marriage. I knew that I wanted children, but I also was afraid. I didn't say anything about these fears to Kendal. I guess because of my brother's problems it was always tucked away in the back of my mind that children are not always born healthy. Further, when I was in tenth grade, I did a research paper on autism. In my research, I ran across a statistic that still haunted me. Siblings of autistic children are 50% more likely to have children with autism than the general public. After we were married a year, my husband began to bring up the subject of children. I was a little hesitant at first, but I really wanted a child. I filed the fears away and said "Okay, let's have a baby."

As it turned out, it took much longer to get pregnant than I had anticipated. In fact, after two and a half years of trying, I decided that Kendal and I would not be parents after all. It just didn't seem meant to be. Shortly after I resigned myself to the fact that I would never have a child, I found out I was pregnant. We were overjoyed. Finally, we would be welcoming a baby into our home. I was busy preparing the baby's nursery and getting fatter every week. It was a very exciting time. All my friends and relatives asked the usual question "What do you want, a girl or a boy?"

I, of course, answered like many people expecting a baby: "Either one as long as it's healthy." For me, this was my deepest wish. I secretly worried about the health of my child. On the day of my first ultrasound, I was excited and nervous. I wanted the ultrasound technician to say that my baby looked healthy and normal. The technician nor my husband were not aware of my concern about this issue. I laid down on the table and lifted my shirt. The technician smeared the jelly-like substance on my belly and rolled the wand slowly over me. She pointed out the baby's heart and other vital organs. She took measurements of the head.

"Do you want to know the sex of the baby?" she asked.

"Yes!" My husband and I answered almost simultaneously.

"It's a little girl."

I was thrilled. I would have a little girl to dress in frilly dresses. My husband seemed pleased although he would have liked a boy, I'm sure. I had a few additional questions I wanted answered. Does she look healthy? I mean does she have all her limbs? Does she have any obvious physical problems? To my relief, she said she looked perfectly normal and healthy.

On the way home I told Kendal I was relieved that she appeared healthy. I told him about my secret fears that I had because of my brother's autism.

"Did you have any concerns about the baby's health," I asked.

"No," he said. "It never even occurred to me that something could be wrong with our baby. But I understand your fears, and I'm glad you told me."

Our daughter Marissa was born via C-section on June 10, 1997. She was a beautiful, healthy little girl. I put most of my fears behind me. I did continue to closely observe her behavior hoping that I would not see any signs of autism. I have since had another beautiful daughter named Meagan. She too seems to be a healthy and intelligent child. Marissa is five, and Meagan is 17 months. I never take for granted their physical and mental health. I'm truly blessed by God.

15
Lessons Learned

It has been twelve and a half years since my brother's institutionalization. I don't get to visit Scott as often as I would like. I still miss him. Sometimes my mind brings me back to a conversation that my mom and I had many years ago. When Scott and I were children, I thought about his future. I told Mom that when she and Dad were gone, I would take him into my home and take care of him. Now he isn't even living in any family members' homes. I've attended church all my life and have a deep faith in God. I believe that God is all-powerful and able to do all things. I reasoned that God could heal my brother if He chose to do so. I prayed frequently for his miraculous healing. Scott remained autistic. I can't say that I understand why, but I don't question the wisdom of God. He sees all and has a perfect plan for everyone that he breathes life into. I was not aware that anyone else in the family had prayed in the same way. Mom and I went on an all-day shopping trip. We used this time to talk about a variety of subjects.

On this trip we discussed Scotty. I said, "You know, Mom, I have prayed many times for Scott to be healed."

She turned and looked at me with a surprised look on her face.

She choked up.

"So have I, Lisa. Many, many times." It's hard to explain exactly how one feels when a family member is mentally handicapped. I felt a desperate need to find a treatment to make life better. If someone told me that running through a burning building would cure them, I venture to say I, like many others, would do just that. I grasped for every straw of hope, never giving up on the fantasy that magically one day my loved one would come back to me.

Scott has adjusted to his life, and his behavior is much improved. I sometimes wonder how different life would have been with a normal brother. Do I wish that he had been normal? Of course, I wanted that, but not so much for my family's sake, but for his. I believe that my brother's life is a gift. Life is full of lessons if we will take the time to examine them and learn. Scott taught me unconditional love and tolerance for people who are different. He taught me that I must live my life to its full potential because I have a healthy body and mind. I'm not sure of all the reasons that my brother has such a debilitating mental illness. I am sure of this one thing. I am honored to be called his sister.

"Scott, I love you."

Afterwards

It has been fifteen years since I first penned these words. Many changes have occurred for both my brother and me. On March 31, 2017, my family celebrated Scott's 50th Birthday at my parent's home. Amazing positive changes have given my brother a home in a less restrictive environment. Approximately seven years ago, an initiative by the Arkansas Governor closed most of the Human Development Centers in the state. My brother's behavior is very stable now. He rarely if ever has violent episodes. He lives in an assisted living center about five minutes from my parent's home in Jonesboro. He has his own apartment with workers supervising him around the clock. He works several days a week at a Sheltered Workshop. He stays with my parents on overnight visits and is at every family holiday celebration. He seems to have a settled peace that I would never have imagined many years ago. He can answer questions appropriately and initiates small conversations. He is definitely able to verbalize his needs and wants. Anytime I see Scott I barely get in the door before he offers a warm hug. He insists on many hugs during my visits, or he acts annoyed. He is able to tell me that he "loves his poor Lisa." I am not quite sure why I am "poor" Lisa, but I'll take it however he wants to say it. When my brother was born in 1967, only 1 in 10,000 children was diagnosed with autism[3]. The last thing I read about it reported that 1 in 54 people is diagnosed somewhere on the autism spectrum[4]. Although that number is not good, I am thankful that more therapies and services are available to people with this developmental disorder and their families. Hope springs eternal that one day a cure will be available. I pray I am alive to witness when that cure is found.

---

[3] The Autism Community in Action.
[4] Autism Speaks organization website

www.ingramcontent.com/pod-product-compliance
Lightning Source LLC
Chambersburg PA
CBHW060353050426
42449CB00011B/2956